适用K-6

tú kǎ 图卡汉语 yì bǎi cí 100词

［汉英对照］

My Magical Chinese World: 100 Chinese Words through Cartoons & Cards

Anita Zhang 编著
郭力 Carlo Reiter 审订

世界图书出版公司
北京·广州·上海·西安

图书在版编目（CIP）数据

图卡汉语100词/Anita Zhang 编著. —北京：世界图书出版公司北京公司，2009.8
ISBN 978-7-5062-9588-8

I. 图… II. 张… III. 汉语—对外汉语教学—教材 IV. H313

中国版本图书馆 CIP 数据核字（2009）第089490号

图卡汉语100词

编 著 者：Anita Zhang
审　　订：郭力　Carlo Reiter
策划编辑：张颖颖
责任编辑：张颖颖
插　　图：星银河 · 张浩洋
排版制作：文辉伟业 悦尔书装

出版发行：世界图书出版公司北京公司
（地址：北京市朝内大街137号　邮编：100010　电话：64077922）
销　　售：各地新华书店及外文书店
印　　刷：北京博图彩色印刷有限公司

MPR 设计制作：天朗闻听
开　　本：787mm × 1092mm　1/16
印　　张：3
字　　数：180千
版　　次：2009年8月第1版　2009年8月第1次印刷

ISBN 978-7-5062-9588-8/H · 1034　　**定价**：98.00元（含1张 CD-ROM）

A Few Words From Amy

 Hello everyone,

I am your friend, Amy! Nice to meet you! This is my dad , my mom , my elder brother , and my lovely friends: handsome , and pretty .

Guess what?

My Magical Chinese World, a **happy** world, can turn daily routines into fun learning adventures for you:

The **Cartoons** can **speak**! Click them on computer 

, touch them in the book 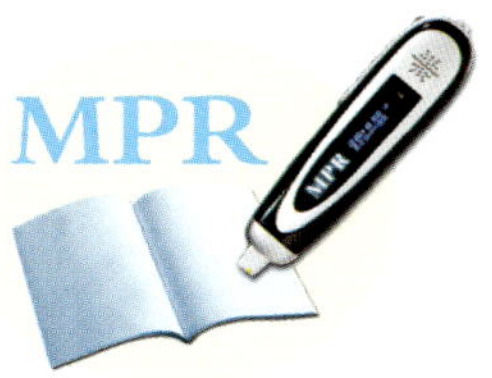

, become friends with them, then enjoy parties with them!

1. Useful sentences and 100 hot words through popular holiday themes.

万圣节

2. Chinese Pinyin with similar English pronunciation, easy to imitate.

3. Hide and Seek. Find the answer in the **Cartoon**.

4. Make a unique mask for yourself! Make something in the **Handcraft Zone**, and attend a party.

5.  Guess what's behind the card? Read The ***Joke of the Day*** in **Magical Cards** for daily laughter!

6. **Magical Stickers** remind you of the most popular sentences!

7. **Fridge Magnets** anxious to decorate your world!

Let's jump into **My Magical Chinese World** together **NOW**!

*Some of the jokes used in this book have been collected from www.kids.yahoo.com/jokes.

Contents

Lesson 第1课 *Look at Me* 我 2

Handcraft Zone

Speaking Puppet 娃娃会说话 4

Cat Puppet 猫咪 7

Lesson 第2课 *Come to My Birthday Party* 来参加我的生日聚会 8

Handcraft Zone

Party Hat 聚会帽 10

Flying Saucer 飞碟 13

Lesson 第3课 *Let's Play Together at School!* 我们在学校一起玩吧! 14

Handcraft Zone

Sock Caterpillar 袜子毛毛虫 16

Clay Caterpillar 粘土毛毛虫 17

Lesson 第4课 *Spring Fun—Garden* 春趣——花园 18

Handcraft Zone

Puppy Fanning Ears 小狗扇耳朵 20

Robin Pal 知更鸟小伙伴 23

Lesson 第5课 *Summer Fun at the Zoo* 夏乐——动物园 24

Handcraft Zone

Monkey Eating Peaches 猴子吃桃子 26

Jumping Frog 青蛙蹦蹦 29

Lesson 第6课 *Halloween is Sneaking up!* 万圣节就要到了! 32

Handcraft Zone

Tricky Box 使坏盒 34

Alien Mask 外星人面具 37

Lesson 第7课 *Merry Christmas!* 圣诞快乐! 38

Handcraft Zone

Christmas Card 圣诞贺卡 40

Family Wish Windbell 家庭许愿风铃 43

gē bo
胳膊
guh bwoh

arm

dù zi
肚子
doo dzi

belly

ěr duo
耳朵
ar dwoh

ear

yǎn jing
眼睛
yahn jeeng

eye

liǎn
脸
lee-yen

face

jiǎo
脚
jee-ow

foot

hǎo
好
how

good

tóu fa
头发
toe fah

hair

tóu
头
toe

head

Lesson 第1课 Look at Me 我

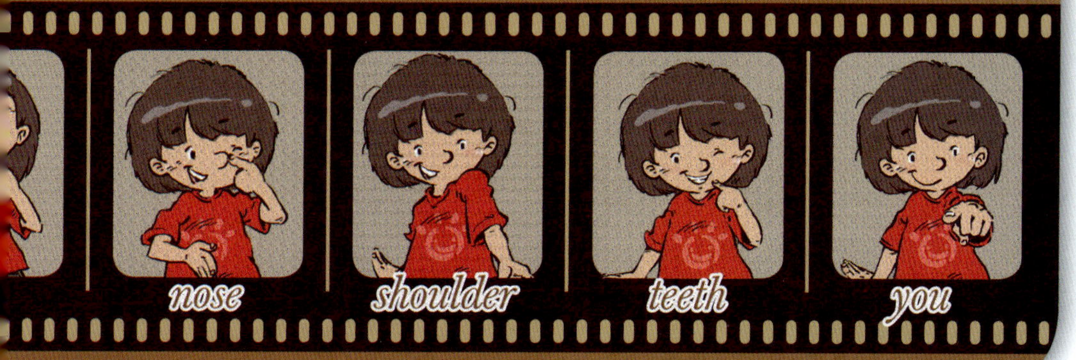

nǐ
你
nee

you

yá
牙
yah

teeth

jiān bǎng
肩 膀
jee-an bahng

shoulder

bí zi
鼻 子
bee dzi

nose

shǒu
手
show

hand

tuǐ
腿
tway

leg

wǒ
我
wo

me

zuǐ
嘴
zway

mouth

bó zi
脖 子
bwo dzi

neck

娃娃会说话
Speaking Puppet

Supplies:
材料

Scissors 剪刀

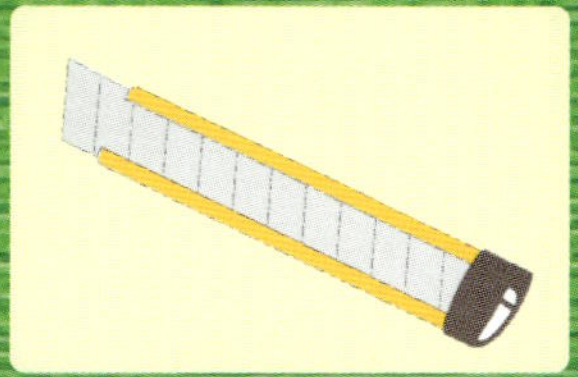

Craft knife 刻刀

Instructions
步骤说明

1. Cut along the edges;
   沿线剪裁；
2. Craft along the two lines of the puppet's face;
   用刻刀沿娃娃脸部的两条线切开；
3. Insert the paper strip into the lines of the face;
   将纸条放入脸上切开的线中；
4. Move the paper strip left and right;
   左右拉动纸条；
5. Now your puppet will speak!
   娃娃要说话了！

TIME NEEDED: Less than 45 minutes
所需时间：少于45分钟

猫咪 Cat Puppet

Instructions 步骤说明

1. Make an enlarged copy of the pattern to fit the tissue rolls;
   把剪纸模型放大到卫生纸卷筒的尺寸；
2. Pin them to the colored paper and cut along the edges;
   把放大的模型订在彩纸上沿模型裁剪；
3. Color in the parts; 给模型上色；
4. Glue on the googly eyes; 把塑料眼睛粘到模型上；
5. Color and distinguish the tissue rolls as head and body;
   分别把头部卷筒和身体卷筒上色；
6. Roll a piece of color paper into a strip to form the cat's tail;
   用一条彩纸卷出尾巴；
7. Paste or tape the eyes, ears, and face onto the head tissue roll;
   把眼睛、耳朵、脸贴到头部；
8. Paste the head tissue roll to the body tissue roll;
   把头部卷筒贴到身体卷筒上；
9. Clamp the body tissue roll with two clothespins as legs;
   用2个衣夹把身体卷筒夹住，作为腿；
10. Create a story about your new cat and tell it to your family and friends!
    给你的家人和朋友讲讲你的新猫咪吧！

TIME NEEDED: Less than 1 Hour
所需时间：少于1小时

Supplies: 材料

2 big colorful clothespins
2个彩色衣夹

Crayons or markers
蜡笔或记号笔

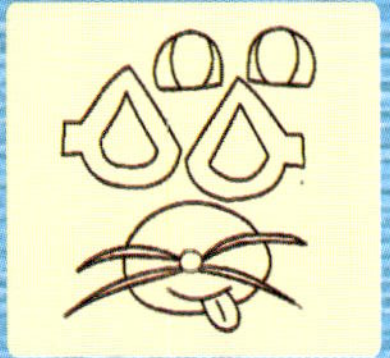

Cat puppet paper
猫咪剪纸模型

Scissors 剪刀

Googly eyes
塑胶眼睛

2 tissue rolls
2个卫生纸卷筒芯

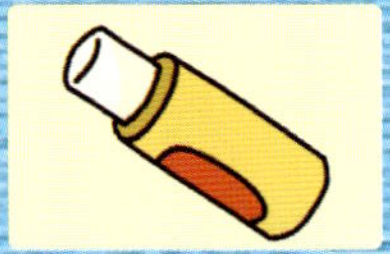

Glue
胶水

Colored paper
彩纸

qì qiú
气球
chee chee-oh

balloon

shēng rì
生日
shung rr

birthday

dàn gāo
蛋糕
dahn gow

cake

Lesson 第2课 Come to My Birthday

chī
吃
chir

eat

gē ge
哥哥
guh guh

elder brother

bà ba
爸爸
bah bah

father

péng you
朋友
pung yoh

friend

shuǐ guǒ
水果
shway gwo

fruit

mèi mei
妹 妹
may may

younger sister

chǒng wù
宠 物
chohng woo

pet

mā ma
妈 妈
mah mah

mother

kuài lè
快 乐
kwai luh

happy

mào zi
帽 子
mao dzi

hat

bīng qí lín
冰 淇淋
beeng chee leen

ice cream

jù huì
聚 会
jooh hway

party

聚会帽

Party Hat

Supplies:
材料

Scissors 剪刀

Glue 胶水

Instructions
步骤说明

1. Adjust the copy to reach the hat size you want to wear;
   把帽子模型的尺寸调整到自己能带上为止；
2. Cut along the edges;
   沿线裁剪；
3. Roll it;
   把帽子卷起来；
4. Glue the marked parts;
   按所示粘贴；
5. Now join the party!
   现在参加聚会吧！

TIME NEEDED: Less than 20 Minutes

所需时间：少于20分钟

TIPS 小贴士

If you want a creative hat, you can decorate the hat with the double-sided tape to attach pom-poms, googly eyes, and feathers.

如果你想做一顶有创意的帽子，可以用双面胶把毛绒球、塑料眼睛、羽毛粘到帽子上哦。

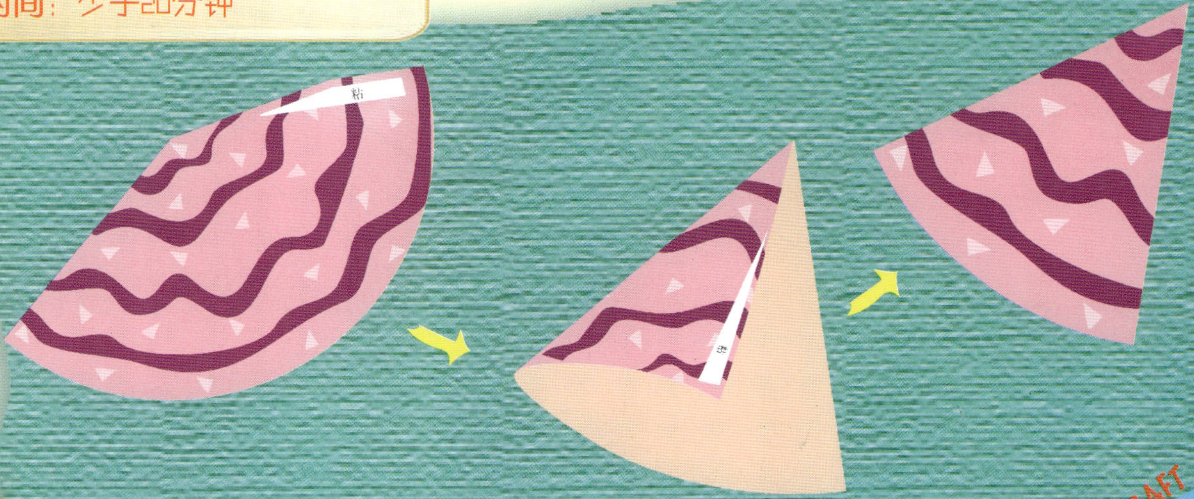

粘

飞碟
Flying Saucer

Supplies: 材料

2 bottle capsules
2个瓶帽

1 jelly cup
1只果冻杯

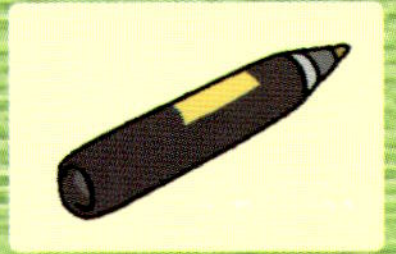

Crayons or markers
蜡笔或记号笔

Scissors 剪刀

Straw pipes
一些吸管

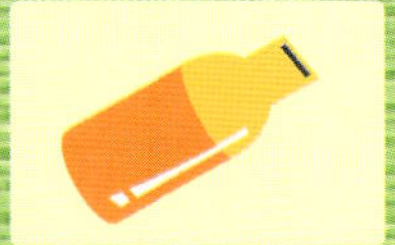

Graft glue
手工胶水

Colored paper
彩纸

Googly eyes
塑料眼睛

Pom-pom
毛绒球

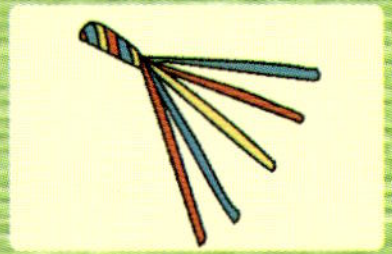

Pipe cleaner
烟斗通条

2 paper plates
2个纸盘

Instructions 步骤说明

1. Glue the two paper plates together along the edges;
   用胶水将两个纸盘沿边粘起来；
2. Fold and glue the straw pipes on the edge of the paper plates as decoration;
   把吸管折一折，并粘到纸盘的边缘，作为装饰；
3. Glue the straw pipes onto the upper paper plate as the antennae; 把吸管粘到上方的纸盘，作天线；
4. Cut a little bit of pipe cleaner as the mouth;
   切一点烟斗通条，作嘴巴；
5. Glue the googly eyes, pom-pom and pipe cleaner on the upper paper plate as eyes, nose and mouth;
   将塑料眼睛、毛绒球和烟斗通条粘到上方的纸盘上，作为眼睛、鼻子和嘴巴；
6. Glue two bottle capsules onto the upper paper plate as ears;
   将两个瓶盖粘到上方的纸盘上，作为耳朵；
7. Decorate the jelly cup with colored papers; 用彩纸装饰果冻杯；
8. Glue the jelly cup onto the upper paper plate as the hat; 将果冻杯粘到上方的纸盘上，作为帽子；
9. Cut the left straw pipes into same length pieces, and glue them onto the bottom paper plate as legs;
   将剩下的吸管切成同等长度的小条儿，粘到下方的纸盘上，作为腿；
10. Visit outer-space with your flying saucer!
    用你的飞碟去外太空看看吧！

TIME NEEDED: Less than 1 Hour
所需时间：少于1小时

Lesson 3 第3课 Let's Play Together at S

shū
书
shoo

book

yǐ zi
椅子
ee dzi

chair

diàn nǎo
电脑
dee-yen now

computer

jiāo shuǐ
胶水
jee-ow shway

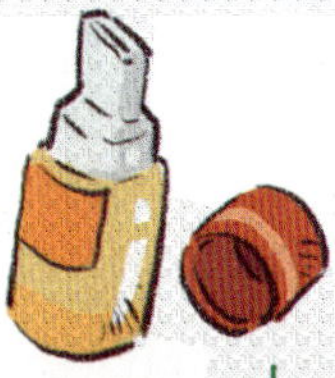

glue

yán liào
颜料
yahn lee-ow

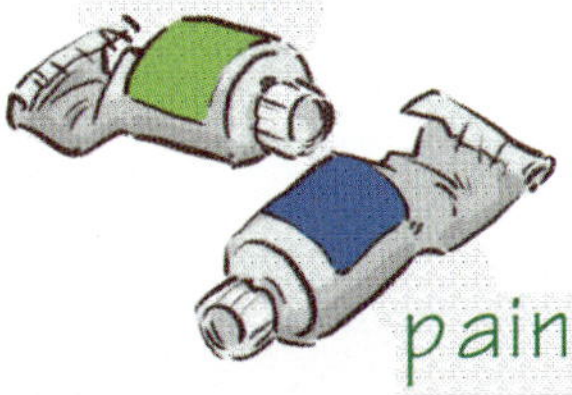

paint

play

huáng sè
黄 色
hwahng suh

yellow

wǒ men
我 们
woh muhn

we

lǎo shī
老 师
lao shir

teacher

án
玩
ahn

xué xiào
学 校
shu-eh shee-ow

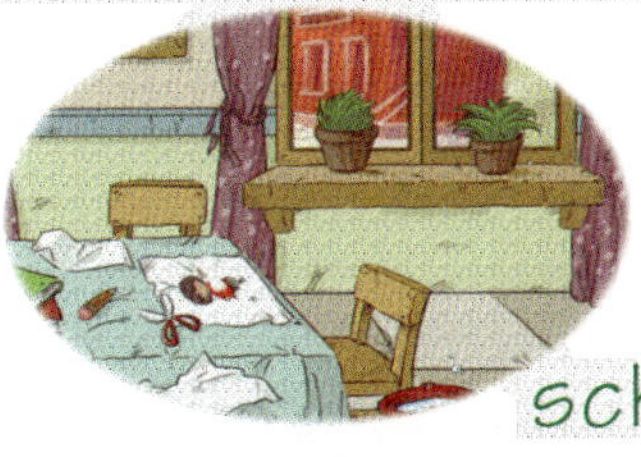

school

jiǎn dāo
剪 刀
jee-yen dow

scissors

袜子毛毛虫

Sock Caterpillar

Supplies: 材料

Googly eyes
塑料眼睛

Crayons or markers
蜡笔或记号笔

Cotton
棉花

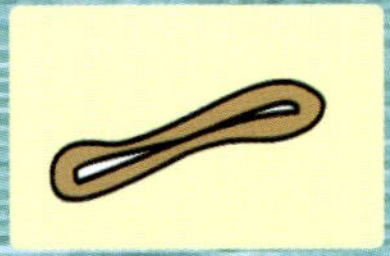

5 rubber bands
5条皮筋

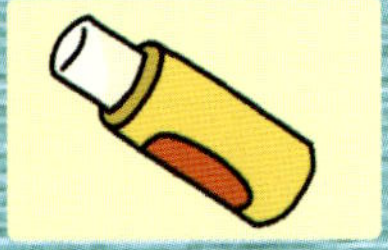

Glue
胶水

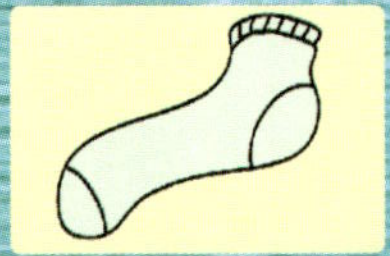

One white athletic sock
1只白色运动袜

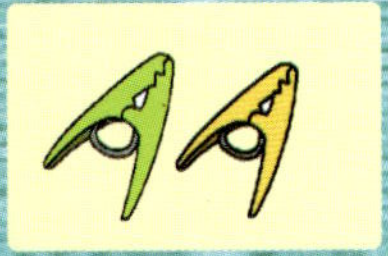

9 small colorful clothespins
9个彩色的小衣夹

TIME NEEDED: Less than 45 Minutes
所需时间：少于45分钟

Instructions 步骤说明

1. Fill the sock with cotton;
   用棉花填充袜子；
2. For the body, band the stuffed sock into 6 pieces with 5 pieces of rubber band;
   用5条皮筋将填充好的袜子绑成6份儿，作为身体；
3. Hide the end of the body; 把尾部藏起来；
4. Glue the googly eyes onto the head; 将塑料眼睛粘到头部；
5. Paint the mouth and body; 给嘴巴和身体上色；
6. Clamp the head as the antennae with 1 clothespin;
   用1只衣夹夹住头部，作为触角；
7. Clamp symmetrically the bottom of the body with the 8 clothespin as legs. 用8只衣夹均匀地夹住身体底部，作为腿。

粘土毛毛虫

Sock Caterpillar

Supplies: 材料

Googly eyes
塑料眼睛

5 rubber bands
5条皮筋

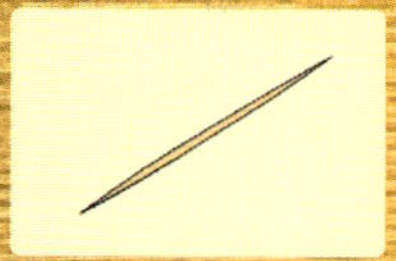

Toothpicks
牙签若干

22-gauge, permanent-colored copper wire
22尺不掉色铜丝

Polymer clay in purple, green, yellow and blue
紫色、绿色和蓝色的粘土

Time needed: Less than 1 Hour
所需时间：少于1小时

Instructions 步骤说明

1. Roll 6 or more colorful balls of clay for the caterpillar body and head;
   揉至少六个粘土彩球，作为毛毛虫的身体和头；
2. String them onto a piece of wire which is long enough to hold them all in place, then bend the body into the shape you want;
   用铜线把彩球串成一排，然后随心所欲地调整身体做造型；
3. For the antennae, roll 2 little balls of clay, and add them to the ends of the wires; 揉两个粘土小球作为触角，按到铜线尾部；
4. Insert the antennae wires into the head; 将触角铜线插到头上；
5. For eyes, press a pair of googly eyes into the head;
   将一对塑料眼睛压到头上作为眼睛；
6. Shape the mouth with the toothpick; 用牙签划出嘴巴；
7. Have a caterpillar party with your classmates!
   和你的同学一起玩毛毛虫聚会吧！

zì xíng chē
自 行 车
dzi sheeng chuh

bike

niǎo
鸟
nee–ow

bird

hú dié
蝴 蝶
hoo dee–yeh

butterfly

Lesson 第4课 Spring Fun—Garden

yā zi
鸭 子
yah dzi

duck

huā
花
hwah

flower

chūn tiān
春 天
choon tee–an

spring

趣——花园

fēng
风
fung

wind

huā sǎ
花 洒
hwa sah

watering can

tài yáng
太 阳
tai yahng

sun

huā yuán
花 园
hwah yoo-en

garden

chí táng
池 塘
chir tahng

pool

zhǒng zi
种 子
dzohng dzi

seed

小狗扇耳朵

Puppy Fanning Ears

Supplies: 材料

Scissors 剪刀

Glue 胶水

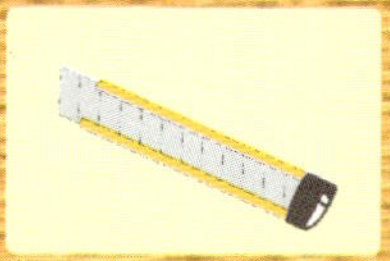

Craft knife 刻刀

Instructions 步骤说明

1. Cut along the edges of the handle;
   沿着手柄图案裁剪；
2. Cut along the edges of the puppy's head, and carve the marked places;
   沿着小狗的头裁剪，并将标示的位置刻出；
3. Fold the head along the dashed line, and insert the handle into the marked places;
   沿着虚线折一折小狗的头，并将手柄插入标示的位置；
4. Set the handle back onto the head, and glue the branches of the handle onto the marked points on the ears;
   将手柄放到头上，并将手柄粘贴到耳朵所示位置；
5. Draw the handle downwards and upwards, then your puppy will fan his ears!
   上下拉动把手，小狗就开始呼扇耳朵了！

TIME NEEDED: Less than 25 Minutes

所需时间：少于25分钟

刻
刻
粘
粘

知更鸟小伙伴

Robin Pal

Supplies: 材料

Scissors 剪刀

Graft glue 手工胶水

Bottle cap 瓶盖

Clay 粘土

Orange paper 桔色彩纸

Googly eyes 塑料眼睛

Orange sock 桔色袜子

Black craft foam 黑色手工泡沫

Red paper 红色彩纸

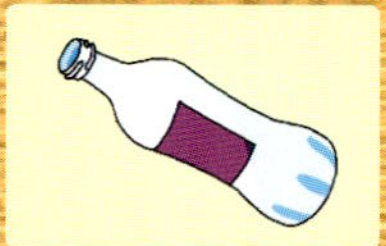
500ml plastic bottle 500ml 塑料水瓶

Rubber band 皮筋

Instructions 步骤说明

1. Fill the plastic bottle with clay to make it stable, then cover it with an orange sock from the bottom;
   为使塑料水瓶固定，可将粘土装进去，然后用桔色袜子从底部把水瓶套住；
2. Twist a rubber band around the bottle neck to hold the sock in place and tuck the top of the sock into the bottle;
   用皮筋将袜子在水瓶口固定住，并将袜子顶部塞进瓶中；
3. From black craft foam, cut a rectangle that wraps three quarters of the way around the bottle and extends about two thirds of the way up from the bottom;
   在黑色手工泡沫上，剪出一个三角形，这个三角形的长度要能绕水瓶一周的四分之三，高度是水瓶高度的三分之二；
4. Trim the edges to resemble robin wings and glue them to the sock;
   修剪知更鸟的翅膀，并将它们粘到袜子上；
5. Cut a beak, a bow tie and feet out of the orange and red paper, and glue them and the googly eyes in place; 在桔色和红色彩纸上，剪出嘴巴、领结和脚，并将它们和塑料眼睛粘到鸟儿的身体上；
6. Top off your bird with the bottle cap hat.
   用瓶盖给你的鸟儿带个帽子吧。

TIME NEEDED: Less than 90 minutes

所需时间：少于90分钟

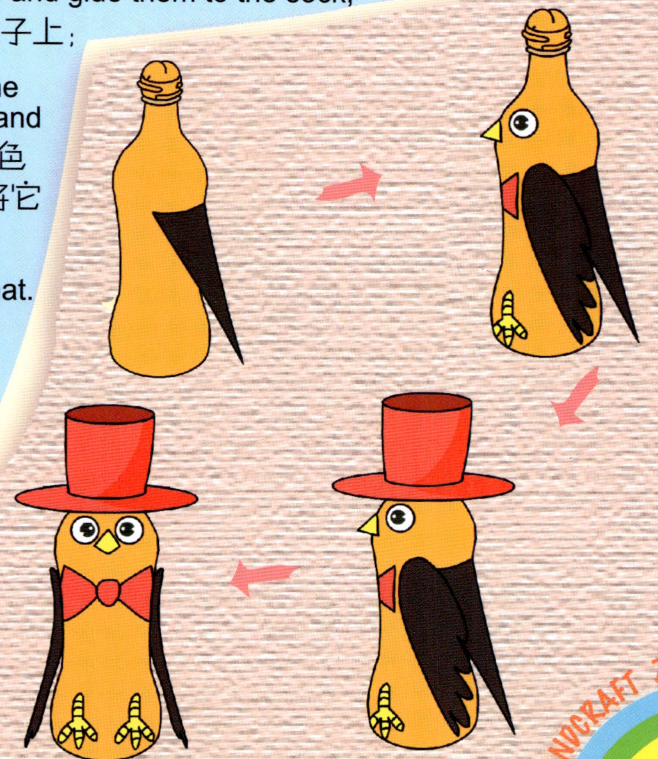

mì fēng
蜜 蜂
mee fuhng

bee

jiǎ chóng
甲 虫
jee-yah chohng

beetle

máo mao chóng
毛 毛 虫
mao mao chohng

caterpillar

dà xiàng
大 象
dah shee-yahng

elephant

Lesson 第5课 Summer Fun at the Zo

dà xióng māo
大 熊 猫
dah shee-yong mao

giant panda

cháng jǐng lù
长 颈鹿
chahng jeeng loo

giraffe

jīn yú
金 鱼
jeen yuu

goldfish

shān
山
shahn

hill

夏乐——动物园

dòng wù yuán
动 物 园
dohng woo
yoo-en

zoo

jīng
鲸
jeeng

whale

shuǐ
水
shway

water

xià tiān
夏 天
she-yah tee-yen

summer

dài shǔ
袋 鼠
dai shoo

kangaroo

shī zi
狮 子
shir dzi

lion

zhī zhū
蜘 蛛
jir joo

spider

猴子吃桃
Monkey Eating Peaches

Supplies: 材料

Scissors 剪刀

Glue 胶水

Craft knife 刻刀

Instructions 步骤说明

1. Cut along the edges;
   沿线裁剪；
2. Glue the monkey onto branch A;
   将猴子粘到A树枝上；
3. Craft the point B on the tree with craft knife, insert the branch A into point B, then glue the leave on the branch A;
   用刻刀在树上B处刻开，并在此处插入A树枝，然后将叶子贴在A树枝上；
4. Draw the branch A up and down, then the monkey will eat peaches.
   上下拉动A树枝，猴子就开始吃桃了。

TIME NEEDED: Less than 25 Minutes
所需时间：少于25分钟

B
A
粘

粘
粘
粘
粘
粘
粘

青蛙蹦蹦

Jumping Frog

Supplies: 材料

Scissors 剪刀

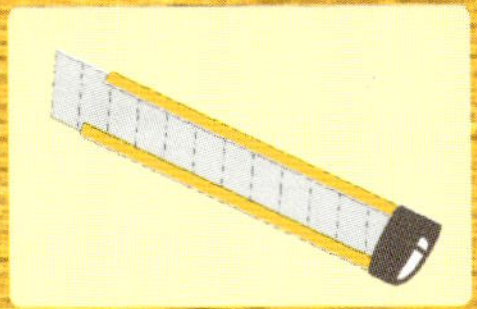

Craft knife 刻刀

Glue 胶水

Instructions 步骤说明

1. Cut along the edges, fold along the dashed line, then glue the tongue onto the upper jaw;
   沿线裁剪，并沿虚线折一折，将舌头粘到上颚上；
2. Glue the upper and lower jaws together according to the pictures;
   如图示，将上下颚粘起来；
3. Glue the body onto the legs, then the frog will jump!
   将青蛙的身体粘在一起，就可以跳起来了！

TIME NEEDED: Less than 25 Minutes

所需时间：少于25分钟

píng guǒ
苹 果
peeng gwoh

apple

hēi sè
黑 色
hay suh

black

táng guǒ
糖 果
tahng gwoh

candy

māo
猫
mao

cat

huà zhuāng fú
化 装 服
hwa jwahng foo

costume

guǐ
鬼
gway

ghost

wàn shèng jié
万 圣 节
wahn shung jee-yeh

Halloween

jié kè
杰 克
jee-yeh kuh

jack-o'-la

wū pó
巫 婆
woo pwoh

witch

qiáng
墙
chee-yang

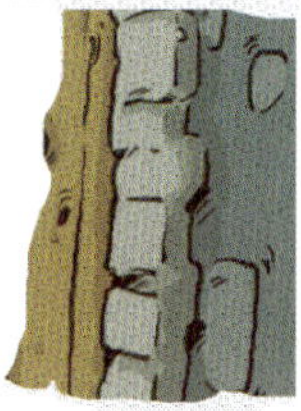

wall

xī xuè guǐ
吸血鬼
shee shway gway

vampire

ng

rn

nán guā
南 瓜
nahn gwah

pumpkin

hóng sè
红 色
hohng suh

red

xiào liǎn
笑 脸
shee-yow lee-yan

smile

kū lóu
骷 髅
koo low

skeleton

使坏盒

Tricky Box

Supplies: 材料

Scissors 剪刀

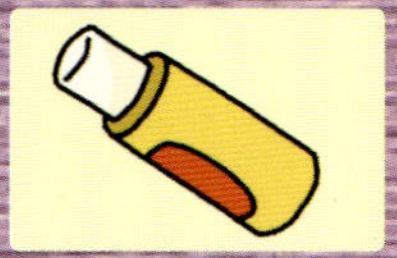
Glue 胶水

Instructions 步骤说明

1. Cut along the edges, and plait the paper strips according to the pictures;
   沿线裁剪，并如图所示编纸辫子；
2. Glue the monster on the paper braid;
   将怪物粘到纸辫子上；
3. Glue the end of paper braid on the box, fold the box, then open it;
   将纸辫子末端粘到盒子上，先关上盒子，再打开它；
4. POP! It's here! 啪！它来了！

TIME NEEDED: Less than 25 Minutes
所需时间：少于25分钟

粘

外星人面具 Alien Mask

Supplies: 材料

1 one-gallon plastic jug 1个1加仑容量的塑料壶

Scissors 剪刀

White Paper 白纸

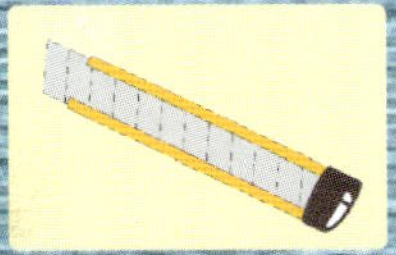

Craft knife 刻刀

Craft glue 手工胶水

Paintbrushes 画笔

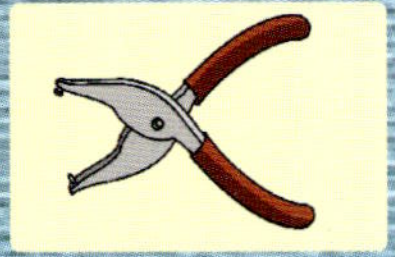

Hole punch 打孔器

Red, green, blue, and white acrylic paints 红色、绿色、蓝色和白色丙烯颜料

2 pieces of 2 foot long yarn 2条2英尺长的毛线

Craft feathers (optional) 手工羽毛（非必备）

Instructions 步骤说明

1. Soak and remove any labels on the jug. Rinse and dry thoroughly;
将壶上所有标签浸湿、撕掉，并洗净、晾干；
2. Cut the jug in half from top to bottom with the craft knife, leaving the handle intact;
用刻刀将壶从上到下一切为二，保留有把手的那一半儿；
3. Hold the handle side of the jug upside down, then cut eye holes in any size you like above the handle(serving as a nose); 将有把手那一半儿口朝下固定住，在把手（面具的鼻子）上刻出眼睛，形状可随心所欲；
4. Cover the entire jug with white paper using the craft glue;
用手工胶水把白纸盖住整个壶；
5. Paint a solid layer with black acrylic paint, ring around the eyes with white acrylic paint, then dot the nose, forehead, and chin with red, green, and blue acrylic paints ;
用黑色丙烯颜料给壶涂层作为底色，用白色丙烯颜料沿眼睛边缘涂色，然后用红色、绿色、蓝色丙烯颜料点出鼻子、前额和下巴；
6. Let it dry; 等它晾干；
7. Punch a hole on the edge of your mask where your ears will be;
依照带面具时你耳朵的位置，在面具边缘打孔；
8. Slip one end of a piece of yarn through the hole you punched and tie it into a knot. Repeat with the other piece of yarn; 将毛线穿过所打的孔，打结；
9. Decorate your mask with the colorful craft feathers;
用彩色手工羽毛装饰你的面具；
10. Here's your alien mask!
你的外星人面具就做好了！

TIME NEEDED: Less than 90 Minutes
所需时间：少于90分钟

Lesson 7 第7课 Merry Christmas! 圣

chuáng
床
chwang

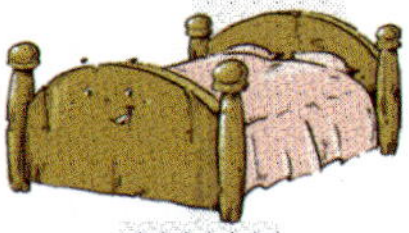

bed

líng dang
铃 铛
leeng dahng

bell

yān cōng
烟 囱
yahn tsohng

chimney

shèng dàn jié
圣 诞 节
shung dahn jee-yeh

Christmas

lù
鹿
loo

deer

bì lú
壁 炉
bee loo

fireplace

lǐ wù
礼 物
lee woo

present

dōng tiān
冬 天
doong tee-yan

winter

chuāng hu
窗 户
chwang hoo

window

shù
树
shoo

tree

shèng dàn lǎo rén
圣 诞 老 人
shung dahn lao ren

Santa Claus

xuě
雪
shu-eh

snow

xuě rén
雪 人
shu-eh ren

snowman

wà zi
袜 子
wah dzi

socks

圣诞贺卡
Christmas Card

Supplies:
材料

Scissors 剪刀

Pen 笔

Instructions
步骤说明

1. Cut the picture of card along the line;
   将卡片中的图片沿线裁剪；
2. Fold its body along the dashed line;
   沿虚线折叠身体；
3. Unfold the picture, and fold along the dashed line;
   展开图片，并沿虚线折叠；
4. Write down or paint your wishes;
   写下或画出你的祝福吧；
5. Hurray! Here it is! 万岁！完工了！

TIME NEEDED: Less than 45 Minutes
所需时间：少于45分钟

家庭许愿风铃

Family Wish Windbell

Supplies: 材料

Scissors 剪刀

Lines 细线

Graft glue 手工胶水

1 round cake box
1个圆形蛋糕盒

Colored Paper
彩纸

Pen 笔

21 spiral shells 海螺壳

Instructions 步骤说明

1. Cut some stars and hearts out of colored paper, glue them onto the round roof of the cake box;
   在彩纸上剪出一些星星和心形纸片，并将它们粘到蛋糕盒的圆顶上；
2. Wash and dry the spiral shells;
   洗净、晾干海螺壳；
3. Punch holes through all of the shells, then bunch them into 6 lines in different length; 将海螺壳打孔并串成长度不同的6串；
4. Make 6 lines through the roof of the windbell and fix up in six different places;
   将6个海螺壳串儿穿过风铃顶部，并固定在6个不同的位置；
5. Cut the paper into strips, write down your family members' wishes on each strip, then insert them into the shells one by one;
   将纸剪成条状，家人各自在纸条上写下心愿，然后将它们分别塞入贝壳里面；
6. Let's bless each other!
   让我们祝福彼此吧！

TIME NEEDED: Less than 60 Minutes

所需时间：少于60分钟

世界图书出版公司北京公司

出创新教材 打特色品牌

对外汉语图书

Books on Teaching Chinese as a Second Language

汉语视听说教程——《家有儿女》

Home with Kids—A Multi-skill Chinese Course

ISBN: (I)978-7-5062-9643-7/H · 1075 (II)978-7-5062-6748-9/H · 1102

Price: 58RMB (DUAL COLOR) /volume; 98RMB (with 2 DVDs) /volume

ISBN: (I)978-7-5062-9551-2/H · 1076 (II)978-7-5062-6750-2/H · 1101

Price: 150RMB (with 2 DVDs) /volume

Features:

• This set of textbooks, which language material is selected from China's top comedy series("Home with Kids"), consists of 3 separate volumes and each volume is composed of 4 individual units. Each unit corresponds to a collection from the play. Each volume is divided into 6 lessons and each is composed of 7 sections: a set of "warm up questions", a text, vocabulary, grammatical points, cultural points, exercises.

• This set of textbooks present the modern Chinese family with humorous and interesting content, the bright and lively language, and derive connotations of Chinese culture from a variety of different angles.

• Each volume is attached with 2 DVDs which consist of the show, vocabulary, and grammatical points.

快乐儿歌——边唱边玩学汉语

Happy Children's Songs—Sing, Play & Learn Chinese

ISBN: 978-7-5062-7659-7/H · 1090

Price: 85RMB (2 books with 1 DVD)

For K-6

Features:

• Animal Pals. The froggie, little monkey, octopus, panda and doggie introduce every section in each chapter, which is very interesting and readable for young learners.

• Play and Learn. There are many handcrafts, puzzles, drawings, and games making learning more interesting and interactive.

• Sing and Dance. There are 12 children's songs in and out of China, easy to learn. The dances in the DVD are designed by professional dance instructors specialized in teaching children and are easy to follow. The cartoons lead the dancing and singing through karaoke videos, which will make the learning experience more interesting.

• Teaching Manual will make teachers and parents really relax in teaching process.

• Colorful layout, Chinese-English bilingual, a free bookmark.